Reginald from Chicago, Illinois, ███ multicompany organization calle███ that encourages teens to stay in ███ drugs, and teaches them how to get jobs. With the latter, I've used quite a lot of your book and thought you should know IT WORKS."

John from Northglenn, Colorado, wrote: I was conservative and only sent out forty Gold Forms, thinking I would send out more later. That was on Friday and Monday I got my first call from an employer requesting more information. I sent that to him but the following Monday I received a call from another employer requesting an interview with me. I was hired and I must say that if I sat down and wrote out a job description of my dream job I wouldn't change a thing. Thanks again Joe and Judy!"

Brad from Littleton, Colorado, wrote: "I was out of college for four months, still no job. Even with a 4.0 and perfect attendance, résumés weren't working. My dad handed me a copy of *How to Get the Job You Really Want and Get Employers to Call You.* He asked me if I was game to try 'something different.'

"On Friday evening I followed the examples in the book and created a Gold Form. I wanted to be a draftsman for an architecture firm. Monday I had twenty-five copies printed on goldenrod paper. I mailed them to the top companies in my field. Wednesday morning I received a phone call for an interview on Thursday. I was offered a job as a draftsman for a large architectural firm and started work the following Monday.

"Seven days from conception to creation of My Perfect Job."

Since 1981 JOE and JUDY SABAH, both of whom have a background in sales, have helped thousands of people find AND get the jobs they really want.

JOE AND JUDY SABAH

How to Get the Job You Really Want— and Get Employers to Call You

A PLUME BOOK

PLUME
Published by the Penguin Group
Penguin Books USA Inc., 375 Hudson Street,
New York, New York 10014, U.S.A.
Penguin Books Ltd, 27 Wrights Lane, London W8 5TZ, England
Penguin Books Australia Ltd, Ringwood, Victoria, Australia
Penguin Books Canada Ltd, 10 Alcorn Avenue,
Toronto, Ontario, Canada M4V 3B2
Penguin Books (N.Z.) Ltd, 182–190 Wairau Road, Auckland 10, New Zealand

Penguin Books Ltd, Registered Offices: Harmondsworth, Middlesex, England

Published by Plume, an imprint of New American Library,
a division of Penguin Books USA Inc. First published by Pacesetter Publications.

First Plume Printing, August, 1992
10 9 8 7 6 5 4 3 2 1

Ⓟ   REGISTERED TRADEMARK—MARCA REGISTRADA

LIBRARY OF CONGRESS CATALOGING IN PUBLICATION DATA:
Sabah, Joe.
    How to get the job you really want—and get employers to call you
/ Joe and Judy Sabah.
        p.   cm.
    ISBN 0-452-26811-7
    1. Job hunting.   I. Sabah, Judy.   II. Title.
HF5382.7.S22   1992
650.14—dc20   92-3936
                                                                 CIP

Printed in the United States of America
Set in Garamond Light
Designed by Eve L. Kirch

First: to my son Joe who asked the *right* question: *"Would you help me get a job, Dad?"*

Next: to my wife, Judy, who asked the *biggest* question: *"When are you going to let the rest of the world in on your 'secret of the Gold Form'?"*

And finally, to the thousands of people who have taken the ideas in this book and proved them successful.

—Joe Sabah

To all people, everywhere, that each may first discover his or her heart's desire, the one thing he or she enjoys doing above all the rest, and that after this discovery, each may become willing to risk and be committed to making that desire the highlight of life. And that this commitment may indeed make this lifetime one of fulfillment and joy.

—Judy Sabah

ACKNOWLEDGMENTS

Our sincere thanks to Margret McBride who believed enough in both of us and our book and new ideas on career change. Because of Margret's vision we will see our goal accomplished: to help tens of thousands of people "sing their song."

Thanks to Winifred Golden and Susan Travis for keeping us "on track" to reach our target date. You both picked up on all the small details that didn't seem important until we saw them in the bigger picture.

Arnold Dolin, New American Library's vice president and associate publisher, must be a visionary. Thanks for being the "Gold Form" type of thinker who is willing to go "beyond the dots" of life. (These special words will only make sense once you've read this entire book.)

Thanks to Carole DeSanti, who is our engineer. Her phone calls and packages became a part of our daily life. Sincere thanks to you, Carole, and your staff who were able to take all the words in our original manuscript and make them meaningful to our readers.

And finally, thanks to over five hundred radio talk-show hosts and their producers across the United States and Canada who have interviewed us. These hosts, producers, and their tens of thousands of listeners have provided us with the ammunition to expand the original ideas and concepts into proven principles. The Gold Form principle is working for thousands who dare to be different, and in doing so are now "singing their song" in their perfect jobs.

Joe Sabah
Judy Sabah

CONTENTS

Part Three—How to Turn Every Job Interview into a Job Offer

Part Four—Success Stories

PREFACE

**If you do what you've always done,
you'll get what you've always gotten.**

How True!

If each of us keeps doing what we've always done—
preparing and mailing out résumés—we will get what
we've always gotten: form rejection letters.

Isn't it about time we started doing something *new?*

In your hands you have what we believe is the first *new*
approach to getting the job you *really want.*

First, a way to help you decide: **What do I *really* want
to do occupationally?**

Next, a new approach and a new alternative to the
résumé that will **get employers to call *you!***

This is a technique that has **not been written about**
in any book on career change, and it is *guaranteed* to
help you **turn every job interview into a job offer.**

At the end of one of our Denver seminars we wrapped
up the day by asking the students for verbal feedback on
what they had gotten out of it. One student and friend,
Tom, closed the seminar with this comment: "You don't

have to be good to start, but you have to start to be good!"
All of a sudden, everyone started writing. Tom asked,
"What did I say? What did I say?"

**You don't have to be good to start,
but you have to start to be good!**

When one of the other students read his comment back
to him he realized the impact of his wisdom.

Thank you, Tom, for reminding all of us to **get started.**
What is it that you want to do?

If we could show you a way to remove all the blocks
in the way of getting what you want, you'd be interested,
wouldn't you?

Let's get started.

Today is the first day of the rest of your life!

It's a new beginning!

Perhaps, up to now, it hasn't been all you expected. Relax . . . with the new day . . . the new life . . . and get ready for new beginnings!

Remember growing up? Did anyone ever ask you what you wanted to be or do when you grew up?

Most of us were told to go out and get a good job and become responsible individuals, and most of us did just that. We looked for a good job that provided what we needed to survive. And many of us are still doing that.

All of a sudden, however, there comes a time in our lives when that's just not enough—when working just to earn a living begins to feel a little like prostituting ourselves. Have you ever wondered, "Is this all there is?" and then answered, "No, there must be more"?

We all have talents—abilities unique to us—that cry out to be expressed. Many times we are not aware of these. We may simply feel that something is not right in our lives. These talents *do* want to be expressed. Depending on the programming we received as children, our feelings about what we want to do may be completely buried beneath a lot of ideas we have heard from others. Our parents, teachers, and peers have been contributing to our programming for many years.

Judy tells about an incident from her life in this way:

I grew up in a small German Catholic community in Kansas. It was quite a strict environment. All of my life I was told what I should do. Today I work very hard at keeping that word "should" out of my vocabulary. I don't ever want to "should on" anyone and I don't want to "be should on" either. However, when I was growing up this environment played a big part in my thinking process. At age eighteen I wanted to enter the sales field and also do some traveling. I was told by those around me that I could not, should not do that. I was a female and it was not appropriate for me to have this type of job. On that basis I decided not to become involved in sales and traveling. The desire to be in that selling and traveling arena never left me, however.

In 1980, twenty-one years later, I had the opportunity to fulfill my desire. Another woman and I went to Miami, Florida, to join a company, selling and traveling. I was overjoyed. Finally my dream could be realized.

Ten days after I arrived in Miami, I was again on a plane, headed back home to Denver. The discovery I had made was this one:

I *didn't like that job at all!*

As I reflect on this incident, I am saddened. Think of all the energy I used in those twenty-one years dreaming about my ideal job. I could have saved that energy and time if I had just done what I thought I wanted to do when I was eighteen. It has become plainly apparent to me that when we have an idea about something we would like to do, the very best thing is to do it. In that way we find out if it is right for us or not. It may be a stepping-stone to something greater, or it could be that through the experience we learn some very valuable information; we may meet someone who is a help to us, or we may find it is the job of our dreams.

On the average, about 65 percent of our population have no idea what it is they want to be doing with their lives. *No one has ever asked them,* and they've never slowed down long enough to ask themselves. *What is it that you want to do?* As soon as you have the answer to that question, you can use some very simple methods to get the job you've *always* wanted.

TGIF—Hump Day—Happy Hour

Do you use any of these phrases? It seems to be an American tradition to recognize TGIF day—"Thank God It's Friday." In fact, if you live in San Francisco your daily newspaper heralds TGIF every Friday on the front page and sets aside a special section to recognize this syndrome.

Have you ever asked yourself, "Why is it that everyone seems to be in a big rush to get through five weekdays so they can enjoy two weekend days?"

And how about Hump Day? Wednesday, of course. You know—"you're over the hump" and "the rest of the week is on the downhill side."

Recently, while giving a talk to a large service club, we asked, "Does anyone know what Hump Day means?" A boy about nine years old raised his hand, exclaiming, "I know, I know—it's Wednesday."

We couldn't help saying to ourselves, "My gosh, we thought that was a World War II term, and here the younger generation is already picking up on it."

And even "Happy Hour" suggests that we can only be happy between 4 and 7 P.M. For sure, only *after* work.

With the constant reminders of TGIF, Hump Day, and Happy Hour, is it any wonder many people are dissatisfied with their jobs? It's as if we're being told that we should not be happy as long as we're working.

Here are three pieces of wisdom that can help break the grip of TGIF, Hump Day, and Happy Hour on your own life.

Play Ball

Does the name Willie Stargell ring a bell?

You'll remember Willie as the captain of the Pittsburgh Pirates major-league baseball team. In the 1970s he helped lead the Pirates to the pennant and several World Series championships. He also had the entire Pirates team rallying around him singing "We Are Family," a song that Sister Sledge made famous.

One day a reporter, interviewing for *Reader's Digest,* asked, "Willie, how do you do it? You're thirty-eight years old and over the hill for a major-league ballplayer. How do you keep on going?"

After a long, thoughtful pause, Willie answered, "I guess you'd have to say: We just listen to the umpire!"

The reporter asked: "What do you mean?"

Willie responded by asking the reporter, "After 'The Star-Spangled Banner' is played, what are the first words from the umpire? *'Play ball!'* "

Willie went on to explain, "We listen to the umpire. *We play ball, we don't work ball.*"

And who are some of the highest-paid people in our society? Baseball players, basketball players, and football players.

Did you notice they're all *players?*

Recently our friend Bob went to Las Vegas. When he came back we asked what he'd done there. He said he had gone to see Stevie Wonder.

Never having seen Stevie Wonder in person, we asked Bob to tell us about him.

Bob replied, "Wow! When Stevie sits down to play the piano the audience goes wild!"

We stopped our friend with the comment, "We're getting the message, Bob. It seems the highest-paid people in our society are those who are *playing.*"

Now, how can we incorporate this idea into our lives, jobs, and careers?

The First Law of Money

Mike Phillips wrote a book titled *The Seven Laws of Money* (Random House, 1974). His book literally jumped off the shelf at us on a recent visit to a bookstore.

Turning to the first chapter, we read the first law of money:

**Money will come
when you are doing the right thing!**

The clearest translation of this in terms of personal advice is, "Go ahead and do what you want to do."

When asked, "What is the most difficult thing for people to understand about money?" Phillips thought about it and came to this conclusion: "The most difficult thing for people to understand about money is *that money will come when you are doing the right thing. Money is secondary to what you are doing.*"

We further believe that the word "right" must be defined very specifically.

With these thoughts in mind, ask yourself, "Am I doing the right thing? What is it that I enjoy doing more than anything else?"

Be Happy

In Richard Bach's words, from his book *Illusions* (Dell, 1979): "Here is a test to find out whether your mission on earth is finished: IF YOU'RE ALIVE, IT ISN'T."

Additionally, from the same book:

"And what would you do," the Master said unto the multitude, "if God spoke directly to your face and said, 'I COM-

MAND THAT YOU BE HAPPY IN THE WORLD, AS LONG AS YOU LIVE!'

"WHAT WOULD YOU DO THEN?"

And the multitude was silent, not a voice, not a sound was heard upon the hillsides, across the valleys where they stood.

And the Master said unto the silence, "In the path of our happiness shall we find the learning for which we have chosen this lifetime. So it is that I have learned this day, and choose to leave you now to walk your own path, as you please."

PART ONE

Deciding What to Do

What Do I Really Want to Do?

If you've ever peeled an onion you've noticed that it is made up of many layers. To get to the middle or heart of the onion, you must peel off layer after layer.

We might think of ourselves in the same way we think of an onion. We have many layers too. Our layers have developed because of years of programming.

As children we expressed our thoughts about what we wanted to do when we grew up. We may have heard comments like "You'll never be able to do that, you're a girl," or "You're not smart enough to do that," or any number of other negative responses. If we believed those comments, and internalized them, that may have been the beginning of our covering up our heart's desire with layers of can'ts or shouldn'ts. This covering up may have continued through our lifetime. We may have gotten involved in doing many types of work that we have not really cared for. It is often mentioned that in the United States, 87 percent of us are unhappy with our jobs.

Some people never, in an entire lifetime, take the time to discover what they really want to do. We have that opportunity now. Why is it so important to accomplish this task? Once we have accomplished it, we have direction. We know what path to take. If we don't know our destination, it is difficult and maybe even impossible to get anywhere.

Now you can begin the process. Reveal to yourself what is most important in your life and then you can begin pursuing it. You can begin "singing the song you came to sing!"

Tools for Finding Our Heart's Desire

Let's begin by completing some projects that can help us to expand our thinking. As we get started, we'll need to remember that if we want to get the most from the projects, we'll have to use our creativity. For some of us that may take a little work.

In the world we live in today, we're not asked to be very creative. As a society we have wanted convenience and ease in doing things. When things are continually done for us, we don't use our creativity. You may have heard the expression "Use it or lose it."

For example, think about our eating habits. In years past, when we didn't have many of the conveniences of today, we thought about what we wanted to eat and about how to prepare it. Today that's no longer necessary.

If you're hungry you can drive down any major street in any city in America and have an overwhelming choice of foods: hamburgers, pizza, tacos, fish, chicken in just minutes. You don't even have to get out of your car.

Or if you prefer you can take advantage of any of the many styles of sit-down restaurants, in any number of price ranges. If you'd rather eat at home you can stop at one of the many supermarkets. They have anything you could ever want. You can pick up a meal from the freezer case and in either your regular oven or a microwave have it ready in a very short time.

The point is, we don't have to think or be creative anymore. It's all done for us.

This is convenient, and it's also allowing us to become very lazy mentally. In order to get at information within ourselves we need to take responsibility for thinking creatively, and, most important, for creating our own future.

COUNT THE SQUARES

The first project to help us do that is called Count the Squares. The objective is to see how many squares you can find.

We want to start looking at things differently. Doing that with this exercise first, we can then use the same basic technique to look at areas of our lives.

As you begin this exercise, get yourself into a relaxed state by sitting in a comfortable position and freeing your mind of any thoughts that are not important to this project.

Look at the diagram of squares that appears here with an open mind, and give yourself at least three opportunities to answer. How many squares do you count?

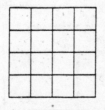

First Answer⎯21⎯Second Answer⎯21⎯Third Answer⎯7⎯

If you said sixteen, you have lots of company. If you said seventeen, you're in a much more select group, but you're still in error. Before you check below to see what the answer really is, why not take another look and see how many more squares you can find?

Why do this exercise?

This exercise will help you expand your mind.

As a result, you will see things differently. You will filter the information that follows through your own value-processing system. You will then be able to apply the information as it is meaningful to you!

And that's the way it should be. You are unique. Protect your uniqueness and allow yourself to be the only person you can be: *you!*

Whether you found sixteen, seventeen, or more squares, promise that you'll always keep an open mind so that you can see yourself and life as they *could* be, and not as they may seem to be.

Now take a look at the correct answer.

As you can see, there are thirty squares. Since you're holding this book in your hands, no one could have added any extra squares. We've simply showed you where they are. This illustrates two important concepts.

First, an in-depth look reveals considerably more than a casual glance, doesn't it? That's true of the squares and it's also true of you, your potential, and your future.

Second, most of us occasionally need someone to point out the obvious, and more often the not so obvious.

Since to educate means to "pull out" or "draw out," the purpose of this book will be to "pull out" the bigger, more capable person in you.

We're convinced you will get a great deal out of this book, but, more important, the book will get even more out of you.

CONNECT THE DOTS

The next exercise is called Connect the Dots.

Again, the purpose is to get you to open your mind. Put your mind to work on this exercise—stretch yourself!

Connect all nine dots, using only four straight lines, without lifting your pencil from the paper or retracing. You get three tries.

Please do *not* read any farther until you've given this exercise three tries. You deserve to get the full benefit of this program by being involved. When you've used up all three tries, turn the page to get the answer.

Did you get the answer on the first try? Congratulations, you're a winner!

Did you have trouble putting your pencil to the paper?

More than 65 percent of us are reluctant to put our pencils to the paper. We've often wondered why. Surely it's not that we're afraid of making a mistake? Or is it a carryover from the days when our teachers and parents told us, "Don't write in the books"?

MORE ON CONNECT THE DOTS

Besides connecting all nine dots with four straight lines, it's also possible to connect the nine dots with three straight lines.

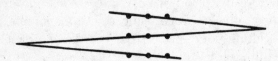

By now, we know, your mind is working.

Recently we challenged some seminar students to connect all nine dots with only one straight line. Jo-Ellen said, "Why not use a three-inch-wide paintbrush?"

Now that's *really* thinking.

How wide is a line? It can be as wide as we want it to be.

Do you remember when you were a kid and your mom gave you a coloring book? What instructions did she give you with the book?

If you had the same kind of mom we had, she said, "Stay inside the lines, honey!"

Now that we're big kids . . . are we still staying inside the lines?

If someone says, "You went outside the lines!", you might ask the question, "What lines?"

Have you heard the story about the mother who gave her three-year-old finger paints for her birthday?

Fortunately, she didn't give her daughter any instructions.

One day the mother walked into the bedroom to find the three-year-old using the finger paints on the wall.

The mother asked, "Honey, what are you doing?"

The child looked up angelically and said, "Mommy, I'm drawing a picture of God!"

The mother responded, "But, honey, no one knows what God looks like."

The little girl replied, "They'll know when I get done with this picture!"

Out of the mouths of babes comes wisdom that we can all use.

Have you asked yourself the question, "Why don't I go outside the lines? Could this be what's keeping me at a job that bores me, or that I've outgrown?"

Let's stop here for a moment.

A student recently asked, "Joe, do you feel that everyone's happiness lies in quitting his or her job?"

Absolutely not!

We believe, though, that it is imperative for each of us to take stock occasionally and *evaluate where we are and where we want to go.* If our job is not helping to take us where we want to go, let's either reexamine the job or reexamine the destination.

Industries change. The buggy whip factory is a thing of the past. When Henry Ford came out with the automobile, buggy whips were no longer needed. The smart people left the buggy whip companies and probably said to themselves, "Now, if we needed buggy whips to start horses, what do we need to start cars?" We can picture these people creating companies like Delco Remy, which manufactures starters, batteries, and spark plugs.

More recently, hundreds of thousands have been employed in the manufacture of computers and hard drives. When it was discovered that this manufacturing could be done less expensively overseas, what did the smart people do? We've seen thousands of small businesses springing up that are creating the software to run these computers. Thousands of other people now operate home-based businesses as consultants to the computer industry.

The key here is not to moan, "My company is cutting back," or "My company is closing down." The key is to ask, "What *else* can I do with my skills and abilities in the field I am already in?"

Besides, changing jobs may not mean changing companies.

A student named Chuck was bored with his job at a large TV station. After being involved in our one-day workshop, Chuck called several weeks later and excitedly said, "Joe, I've got a new job."

Joe said, "Great, Chuck! Where are you working now?"

Chuck replied, "No, Joe. You weren't listening. I didn't

change companies. I just changed jobs. I'm still with the same TV station."

After more questioning, Chuck explained that he had used the ideas from our jobs seminar and decided to go to his boss with his problem. His boss said, "Why didn't you tell me you were bored before, Chuck? We need someone with your ability over in another department."

As a result of this conversation, two people are happier: Chuck, who has newfound freedom of expression in his new job, and his boss, who solved two problems: keeping a valuable employee at the TV station and filling an open job with a person who had experience and was loyal to the station.

Chuck went outside the lines by being honest with his boss about his boredom.

And just what is this fear that keeps us from going outside the lines? Could it be the fear of failure, or is it the fear of rejection?

The Greatest Fear

The People's Almanac Presents the Book of Lists (Morrow, 1977) catalogued the ten greatest fears people have. It listed things like flying, falling, and speaking before groups.

We believe it left out the number one greatest fear that most job hunters face.

Yes, it's the *fear of rejection*.

If the question is, "Why don't we just go out and offer our services to an employer?", the answer seems to be, "Fear of rejection!"

In a job search, we may make one or two calls. If any of these calls results in a turndown (for *any* reason), the big fear of rejection raises its ugly head. And before we allow ourselves to be turned down again . . . we head for the safe, protected environment of home.

And to protect ourselves even further we use phrases like

"Nobody's hiring!"
"I'm overqualified!"
"I'm underqualified!"
"I'm too old!"
"I'm too young!"

Where did all this fear of rejection start? Perhaps it can be traced all the way back to grade school. Remember your first dance? The boys stood on one side of the room and the girls on the other. Next the teacher said, "Johnny, why don't you go over and ask Mary to dance?"

Do you think Johnny was about to risk getting turned down?

And so it began. Slowly at first, we protected ourselves against the fear of rejection by *just not risking*. And by not risking we stay in a "comfort zone" that does not allow us to experience what we call *really living*.

Now that our minds are starting to open, we want to continue the process.

Finding out what we want to do is not a one-time event. We must realize that it's a process.

Change—The Only Thing We Can Really Count On!

We're constantly changing throughout our lives—our values, our ideas of what we want, of where we are going. Have you noticed that some of the friends you had several years ago are no longer in your life? If you're like us, every year you update your address and telephone books. How many names get left behind! These names represented significant relationships when we entered them in our books. Now their owners have either moved out of town or moved out of our area of interest.

Think about "things" for a few moments. Have you ever moved from a large house to a town house? From a small car to a larger one? During the past five years we've moved from a four-bedroom house to a two-bedroom apartment back to a four-bedroom house. Our needs keep changing. How about yours?

Nothing remains the same. The sooner we realize the truth in that statement, the more we'll be in the flow of life.

Now we want to experience "going outside the lines." We deserve to live the fuller life, and from this day forward we will do everything that will lead us to total fulfillment and accomplishment.

Getting in Touch

Understanding our feelings is vital to knowing where we want to go. As we learn to get more in touch with our feelings, they will function just like a road map.

The next exercises have been created to help you to do just that.

EXERCISE #1: PEAK EXPERIENCES

Stop. Listen to yourself . . . and think about the peak experiences you've had in your life so far. A peak experience is one that stands out in a positive way, one that you would enjoy reliving over and over.

You may be able to describe your peak experience in a few words, or it may take several sentences. Your peak experience may involve a volunteer job you once had or some episode from your personal life. Don't concern yourself right now about anything except sorting out experiences that left you with *good feelings!*

Here's an example from Joe's life.

When I was twenty-six I had the opportunity to go through the Dale Carnegie Course while living in Steubenville, Ohio.

Part of this class involved overcoming the "fear of speaking." As a result of fourteen weeks of constantly practicing speaking before an audience, I became addicted. My career in the life insurance industry was enhanced as a result of my improved speaking skills. I went from a top-producing sales agent to manager to assistant superintendent of agencies.

My next career move found me using my speaking skills more and more. In fact, I believe that our jobs seminar was a direct result of my getting hooked on speaking.

Now I have to admit, *I'd rather speak than eat*—and I love to eat!

Think back to the peak experiences you've had—experiences that left you on a high, things you would love to do over and over. List as many of these experiences as possible. Don't try to analyze them. Keep on writing.

Peak Experience #1

_____

_____

_____

Peak Experience #2

_____

_____

_____

Peak Experience #3

_____

_____

_____

Peak Experience #4

_____

_____

_____

Peak Experience #5

_____

_____

_____

Peak Experience #6

_____

_____

_____

Do you find a common thread connecting any of these experiences?

Did these experiences involve people or things? The indoors or the outdoors? Kids or adults?

EXERCISE #2: I'VE ALWAYS WANTED TO BE A _____

Think back on your life so far. Have you ever said, "I've always wanted to be a_____"?

Now, without allowing any restrictions or reasons why you can't be a_____, here's your chance to honestly finish the sentence.

Ask yourself this question: "Am I doing what I've always wanted to do?"

If not, you may want to ask yourself another question: "What stands between my doing what I'm doing today and my doing what I've always wanted to be doing?"
Answer:

_____

_____

_____

Now for the *biggie!*

Are you willing to pay the price to have your life be the way you really want it? You need to remember that there is a price for everything in life. If you stay in the circumstances you're in now, the price could be your life itself. Serious illness can come from the stress of being in a job you hate. Take the time to consider the price you're paying now for what you have in your life.

For example: Do you need *further education* to qualify for your perfect job? Are you *willing to relocate* for the right job? How can you get the education you need or make the move?

Is it *more experience* that you need?

Do you need to get yourself into a *more financially secure position?* How much money would you need to have in the bank to feel secure about making a change?

Are You Willing to Pay the Price?

The price for making this change is:

_____

_____

The highest price that most people have to pay for their perfect job is either reeducation or relocation.

And remember, it's only *your* answer that counts! You are unique! Only *you* can decide what it is *you* want to do!

EXERCISE #3: CASUAL COMMENTS

Have any of your friends or relatives ever said this to you?

"You're really good at _____."

Has more than one person said that to you? More than two people?

Why do you think other people see that special something in you? Could it be the direct result of the energy and enthusiasm you put into certain activities?

Can you see that special something in yourself?

This is a most valuable area to follow up. You may want to invite a good friend to have a cup of coffee or a soft drink with you. During the conversation, you'll want to ask questions like "What qualities do you see in me that really stand out?" "What traits or characteristics do you see in me that are really marketable?"

Just let the conversation go along naturally and be observant. Bring paper and pen, as you'll want to make notes of the ideas that flow.

Now, get ready for an interesting experiment called the Banner Project. This project will help you to "take a picture of your own mind."

EXERCISE #4: BANNER PROJECT

With this exercise you'll create a lasting visual image of what you're thinking about *today!*

Start by writing down today's date: __/__/__

Remember, this Banner Project, when completed, will show what we'd have if we could "take a picture of your mind" today.

This doesn't mean you'll stay the same forever. So, when you do the Banner Project again in six weeks or six months, the picture will change. If you don't believe that, think about your high school graduation picture. How does it compare with the way you look today?

With this as a reminder, allow yourself to recognize how you feel today and remember that you can change your banner from time to time. Nothing that you'll do in this or any of the other exercises in this book is etched in granite. These exercises are only pencil or ink on paper, both of which can be erased or written over.

Following the "key," use a word, short phrase, or symbol to describe yourself according to the questions below and write them on the diagram on page 30. You may want to refer to the impressions you wrote down about yourself in the previous exercises.

Key

1, 2, 3, 4: Create four symbols (pictures) that represent your deepest, most cherished values in life. Do these in order of importance (1, 2, 3, 4).

Use written statements (short phrases or words) to answer the following:

5. Who am I?
6. What has been my happiest moment or experience or greatest achievement?
7. What are three things I do well?
8. What three areas, characteristics, or attitudes do I want to improve?
9. What is a personal motto by which I (try to) live?
10. What one thing would I like to have said of me if I died today?

11. What three things would I like to learn to do well?
12. What three accomplishments do I want to realize during my lifetime?
13. What three things would I like to start doing now?
14. What are my three highest-priority life goals?

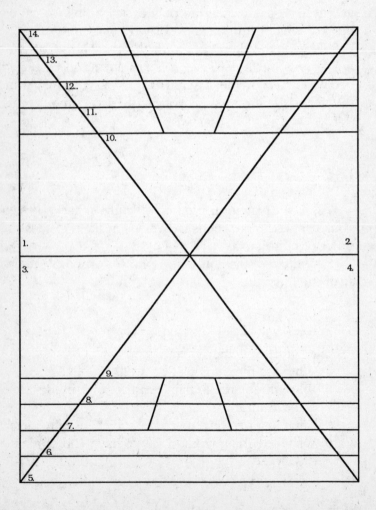

Once you've completed the Banner Project, you'll want to take time out to analyze your responses to each question.

We believe that the answer to question 6, "What has been my happiest moment or experience or greatest achievement?", could be the beginning of a more thorough search into your career wants.

Question 7, "What are three things I do well", could lead you to your real strengths. For example, if a baseball player is a good pitcher, we doubt the manager would also ask him to catch or play outfield. The pitcher keeps practicing what he is already good at . . . and as a result *gets better*.

If a singer has discovered that she is a great soprano, no singing coach would have her practice being a tenor. The key is to *get better* at what we're *already* good at.

Continue studying your answers to the Banner Project and you'll keep having those wonderful revelations sometimes known as "aha" experiences.

EXERCISE #5: JOURNAL WRITING

Another great way to get in touch with your thoughts and feelings is to start keeping a journal. Using a notebook, start writing every night before going to bed, putting down all the thoughts and feelings that are going on inside you. Get these thoughts and feelings on the outside. The wonderful thing about a journal is that it is nonjudgmental. We all need to talk about what's going on inside us, and often it's impossible to find someone who will listen. Your journal will listen to you forever.

The next step is to begin to write down your thoughts and ideas about the kind of job you would really like to be involved in. Write down all the details about this job. Use all the information you've compiled from the other exercises you've done to this point. Think about how you would feel being in the job, what the salary would be—every detail. Write and rewrite this description until it becomes crystal clear.

EXERCISE #6: SETTING YOUR PRIORITIES

At this stage of your search for your perfect job, it's also a good idea to begin analyzing your priorities. Take a large sheet of paper and cut smaller pieces from it, about two by three inches. You'll need eight to ten small slips of paper. On each of the slips, write down a word or phrase that describes something that's important to you in the job you want.

The words and phrases could be some of these:

money
security
benefits
freedom
flexibility
environment
closeness to home
rapport with supervisors
atmosphere
recognition

You'll also have some words of your own that pertain to your particular life-style. When you've finished, start putting the slips of paper in order of their importance to you. What's the most important item on your list? Next, arrange the slips of paper in a column with the most important one at the top. Arrange and rearrange them until you're satisfied that the most important item is number one on your list. Take your time; you're finding out what the most important things in life are for you.

The information you'll gain from these exercises is invaluable. As you gather it, you'll find it will help you on the next project.

The Myth of Newspaper Want Ads

All our lives we've used the want ads in the newspaper as our source for job hunting. We've believed that the answer to our job hunting problems lies in those ads. Friend, this is not true. Many times the job you see advertised in the paper is filled before the paper hits the streets.

Why? Because employers need to fill openings immediately. As soon as it looks as if a spot will open up, discussion begins about "who knows who" and how to reach that person so the spot can be filled. However, the employer generally puts an ad in the paper because it has always been done that way.

The point is that the want ads are not the answer. *Only 5 percent of all jobs filled are filled through WANT ADS.*

Another peculiar feature of want ads is that the person writing the ad believes that certain education and experience are necessary for the position—but have you ever applied for a job and then found out that the person who got it did not have the requirements that were listed in the want ad? Yes, it happens.

The ads in the paper give us the feeling that someone else controls our future. *We* need to *feel* and *be* in control of our future. We can, however, use the want ads to our advantage.

EXERCISE #7: WRITING YOUR PERFECT WANT AD

Pretend with us for a few minutes.

Pretend that you have the morning newspaper in front of you and you're going down the want ad columns. You're circling the ads for jobs that you believe you're qualified for.

All of a sudden you come to *the perfect want ad.* It has the right salary, the right location, the right duties, the right responsibilities. *Everything* is perfect.

What would that ad say?

Either in the space provided here or on a blank sheet of paper, start composing your Perfect Want Ad.

MY PERFECT WANT AD

_____

_____

_____

_____

_____

_____

_____

_____

_____

_____

_____

_____

_____

_____

_____

_____

_____

_____

_____

_____

Make sure your Perfect Want Ad includes *all* the details. These details should include the answers to the following questions:

Where would I be working (city and state)?
What would I be doing (very specifically)?
Who would I be working for (the size and type of company)?
Who would I be working with (the types of people)?

Be very specific. The more specific you are the easier it will be to visualize *your perfect job.*

Since there's no charge for this want ad, use as many words as you need. Be very clear about what you would be doing in your Perfect Job. And fill in the details about everything surrounding it: the atmosphere, the office decor. What sounds would you hear as you worked at this job? Use your other senses too. Would there be a smell associated with your new environment? How about taste? How would you feel as you went about your work?

Some time ago we held a full-evening seminar called "How to Get the Job You *Really* Want" and included this exercise. At the seminar was a young fellow named Bruce. Bruce worked for a large downtown bank and came to the seminar in his pin-striped suit, really looking the part of a banker.

As Bruce started writing his Perfect Want Ad he began to giggle. Joe asked, "What's so funny?" Then he asked Bruce to read what he had written so far.

Bruce read, "I'd like to be the marketing director for the Barefoot Cruise Lines in the Bahamas." Then he started to giggle again.

The seminar participant sitting next to Bruce chimed in: "What's so funny, Bruce? Somebody's got to do it!"

Guess where Bruce was going on his next vacation? He was taking a week off and going on a Barefoot Cruise in the Bahamas. What a way to check things out! He was going to do it in person.

There's a valuable lesson for all of us in this:

Try it—you may like it!

When we gave a couple of talks to two groups of high school seniors several years ago, we found an example of how different we all are in our desires.

We were to talk about job hunting; but that doesn't mean the same thing to all people. There were about twenty-five students in each group. In preparing for the talks, our first question to ourselves was, "How can we reach these individuals and hold their interest?" We began by asking them questions about what they wanted, what their interests were.

The first group of students was interested in how to find a job with security and benefits. Retirement was important to them. The second group was looking for satisfaction and fulfillment. Their ideals were much loftier.

Finding out exactly what *you* want from a job is a vital part of the whole process. After you've finished this project, review your Perfect Want Ad regularly to see what changes you need to make. Spend as much time as necessary on the project—it's a big part of the search for satisfaction in your life.

IFI—Interviewing for Information

Let's assume that you've made a decision about your Perfect Job. Now you'd like a little more clarity. Here's the best way to gather more information about the particular area you're interested in: Interviewing for Information. Using this method, you can find out anything about any subject you want.

This project could also be called "Learning to Ask Questions."

Find three people who are now doing whatever it is you want to be doing. Phone each of these people and invite him or her to go to lunch with you—not a short lunch, but one that can last two or two and a half hours. This is an interviewing lunch. The reason you're calling *three* people is that you need to be able to compare their ideas and come to your own conclusions.

Why, you ask, would these people want to go to lunch with you to give you information? Simply because you'll be asking them about their favorite subjects: themselves and what they're involved in. They'll be happy to tell you all the details, if you'll only ask.

Here's the scenario: "Hi, Janie, my name is Judy Smith. I understand you are in the public speaking business, is that right? Janie, I've been thinking about getting into that field. I'm looking for someone who could tell me a little about the business from her point of view. I'd like to take you to lunch so we could share some ideas on this subject. Would you have some time Tuesday, or would Thursday of this week be more convenient?"

We promise that Janie will be delighted with Judy's invitation. It's been our experience that Janie will be complimented and eager to share information and her ideas, which of course she thinks are the best in the world.

What stops us sometimes from Interviewing for Information is that we're afraid to pick up the phone and make that call. We human beings suffer from two terrible fears: fear of rejection and fear of inadequacy. What if the person says no, or what if I don't have the right questions to ask and the person thinks I'm dumb? "What if" has killed more good ideas and kept more people from success than anything else, with the exception of "What will other people say?" and "What will other people think?" They won't say or think anything; they're too busy thinking about their own lives.

Interviewing for Information can get us any information we want. The problem is, we've never been taught to ask questions. We think we should only give answers.

The most important lessons we can learn are to *ask questions* and *always answer a question with a question*. Start practicing this right away. Start with your own family. This will work for you beautifully.

Here's a letter we received from a woman named Lynn about her personal experience in Interviewing for Information.

Dear Joe and Judy,

The first advice I took was to write and rewrite a description of the job, the perfect job for me. The more I wrote the more I saw four elements: researching, writing, social services, and politics. But how to combine these?

So I took the next logical step, also at your advice, and began to call people. I can never describe the fear and trembling I felt at taking so bold a step—and yet I managed to dial the numbers after many false starts.

After three very enjoyable—and not so expensive— lunches (I spent considerably less than I would have paid an employment agency), *I landed the job of my dearest dreams, at twice the money I earned at my last position.* Beginning Monday, I will be doing research and writing for a professional lobbyist who has mostly social service agencies as clients.

For two months, I must confess, I had my doubts about your approaches. In my weaker moments I actually resorted to the want ads rather than talk to anyone I didn't know over the phone. But the rejections that came in the mail without my ever stepping foot in an office could not compare with the relaxed, enjoyable, and informative meetings I had with these three professionals. All were delighted at the chance to talk about their work and to help me focus on my goals. The third actually fashioned a job from the description of both of our needs.

I want to thank you for sharing these techniques and especially for your ability to make your students feel special, capable, and fully entitled to their dreams.

Love,
Lynn

Can you imagine? Through the process of Interviewing for Information (not asking for a job), Lynn actually got what she wanted. And at *double* her previous salary!

What questions did she ask?

Here's how to make your interview a successful one. With a pad in hand, make a list of questions, such as:

"How long have you been in this business?"
"How did you get involved?"

"What are the requirements of your position?"

"How much education did you need?"

"Are you happy doing this?"

"What do you like most about your business?"

"Do you see this field as being on an upswing or a downslide?"

"If you had it all to do over again, would you do the same thing?"

Open-ended questions like these will get a person talking for long periods.

As the person talks, give him or her your full attention; be a good listener. Make notes. This is a further compliment to the person, and you'll have the information for later use.

The rest of Lynn's story is that as she was interviewing that third person, the executive director of a lobbying organization that worked with social service agencies, the woman suddenly said to Lynn, "I don't know why I'm spending so much time here at lunch; I have so much work to do. In fact, I need a person just like you. A person who can do writing and research for us." That was when she wrote Lynn's job description on the back of a napkin.

Lynn had found this person by going to the Yellow Pages.

The Yellow Pages Are Where All the Jobs Are!

She looked under the list of associations of the type she thought would do the kind of work she was interested in doing. (We'll tell you more about using the Yellow Pages, as well as specialized directories, in Part Two.)

In one of our classes a student named Margie expressed interest in the field of training. We referred her to the Yellow Pages where she found the Rocky Mountain chapter of the American Society for Training and Development. We advised her to attend one of their meetings, which she did. Not knowing anyone there, she sat down and introduced herself to the first person she met. When her "dinner mate" asked, "And what do you do?" Margie answered, "I'm looking for a job as a trainer." Her new friend responded, "You can't have my job, it's already taken." During dinner Margie questioned her new friend about the opportunities in the field of training. They exchanged names and phone numbers. About three weeks later Margie received a phone call asking if she'd be interested in a part-time training position. You can imagine the rest of the story: Margie's part-time position turned into a full-time position. She now has her Perfect Job all because she learned to Interview For Information.

It's very simple. If you want information on bartending, ask a bartender or an instructor at a bartending school. On real estate, a realtor; on nursing, a nurse. It's called "getting it straight from the horse's mouth."

But sometimes we still get mixed up—like asking a brother or neighbor what he or she thinks about a particular job. How can a truck driver tell anyone what it's like to be a CPA, or an advertising copy writer explain the job of a chef? We just need to remember to go directly to the people who can give us the information from their own experience.

In Summary

Finding the answer to the question "What is it that I would like to do occupationally?" is the ultimate. Some people never find that answer. They never are able to "sing the song they came to sing" and sometimes go to their grave with the music still inside them.

After you've completed the exercises and projects in this book, you'll have a clearer idea of your "song." If your vision of your "right work" doesn't come with the first exercise, keep working at it. The answer is inside you. Looking for that ideal job is a full-time job in itself.

If you hold a magnifying glass in one spot over a piece of paper with the sun shining on it, the paper soon catches fire. But if you move the magnifying glass around, the sun never focuses on one spot long enough to start a fire.

The same idea applies when we're going after something as specific as a job. We need to focus our attention on the project—to limit our thinking to that project. The more we focus, the sooner we'll get results.

PART TWO

How to Get Employers to Call You

Down with Résumés!

For many years people have used résumés to get jobs. And many times this method has proved ineffective. We may spend hundreds of dollars to create the perfect résumé; then we send them out, only to find that many of them have gone into the round file or the personnel file, leaving us with nothing but a form letter.

Recently we interviewed an owner and manager of a radio station in Kansas City. We asked, "Do you ever get any résumés in the mail?" He replied, "You bet. I get three or four a week."

Our next question: "What do you do with these résumés?" His reply: "I send them a form letter in response."

We should have known better than to ask the next question: "Why?"

His answer: "Well, they send me a form letter, so I send them a form letter." Touché—a standoff, wouldn't you agree?

Why are résumés ineffective?

Résumés always talk about the past. Employers want to
know what you can do today that will help them to make
more money so that it's worth paying you. That's the
bottom line. Résumés do not give the employer that information. Granted, some employers still request a résumé.
There are companies that won't make a hiring decision
without having a résumé in the files. If you know for sure
that that's the case, then, yes, you do want to supply a
résumé. Before you get too far ahead of yourself, however, you want to market yourself in a positive, nontradi-
tional way to get results.

This is called selling yourself—advertising the best
product you have to offer.

Get Employers to Call You—Yes, You Can!

If you could find a way to reverse the job hunting situation and have employers call you, how would you feel
about that? You'd feel great, wouldn't you?

What follows could well be the most valuable section
of this book.

We've been told that the ideas presented in this section
are *new* to the changing career field and may well revolu-
tionize the job search of the future.

People who have learned about our "Gold Form" and
followed our instructions for using it have *all* had employers call them. And better still, the results have been

consistent: people write and call to tell us, "I now have the job I *really* want!"

May we first tell you how this Gold Form came about? As the story unfolds, picture yourself in the same situation. You'll want to be thinking about the question "How can I apply this to my situation?"

This story comes directly from Joe.

In 1977 my son Joe, living in California, had just turned eighteen and graduated from high school. Calling him from Colorado and congratulating him on his accomplishment, I asked, "What can I help you with, Son?"

Without hesitating, he replied, "Help me get a job, Dad." I asked him what he wanted to do. He answered, "I want to be a printer, Dad."

I asked him why. He told me that he had completed a graphics class in high school, and went on to list the types of presses, cutters, cameras, etc., that he could operate.

I said, "Joe, may I call you back in an hour?"

Then, going to my typewriter, I sat down and let my fingers put on paper the ideas that flowed from my mind.

An hour later I called Joe and said, "How does this sound, Son?" I read to him exactly what I had typed (see Joe's Gold Form on page 108).

When he finished laughing he asked, "What are you going to do with that, Dad?"

I replied, "I have a copy of your Concord, California, Yellow Pages in front of me, and there are thirty-seven print shops in your town."

Like an eighteen-year-old, he said, "So?"

I went on, "I'm going to have this printed and mail one to each print shop in Concord. I just have a feeling that several of them need printers."

Joe answered, "Do you realize how much postage that's

going to take?" (Do you remember thirteen-cent stamps? That's how much postage cost in 1977.)

I answered, "Joe, look, I'll take care of the postage; I just want one promise from you. And that is that you will be there to answer the phone when it rings."

Joe asked, "Honestly, Dad, do you expect anyone to call me with a job offer?"

"Of course I do!" I answered enthusiastically. (It's called Positive Expectancy. Here's what we mean by Positive Expectancy: There is a law called Law of Attraction. When we believe that good things or positive things will happen to us, that is most often what we get. The same of believing that negative things will happen to us. You may have heard it as "Like attracts like.")

Joe promised he would be there to answer the phone.

On Thursday I took the form to a local print shop and asked the clerk for thirty-seven copies. She asked, "What color paper do you want it on?" I responded, "What is the brightest color you've got?" She told me, "Goldenrod." I said, "Why not? Let's go with it!"

I didn't realize the impact of color, especially goldenrod, until much later. So I addressed envelopes to the thirty-seven print shops and mailed out the goldenrod forms on Thursday.

On Tuesday of the next week, Joe called me and said, "Guess what, Dad? I got replies from three print shops who want to see me."

Now, Joe might have told me that he got turned down thirty-four times. But he didn't hear from the other thirty-four print shops, so we will never know, will we?

I could just as easily have told Joe to personally visit thirty-seven print shops and tell the managers, "Here I am, ready to go to work for you!" But, honestly, do you think Joe would have made those thirty-seven personal visits?

Let me ask it this way: Would *you* have made thirty-seven calls?

Probably not. It's back to the basic fear of rejection that we allow to creep in. But this is a different story, since three shops called Joe and said, "We want to talk to you about printing for us."

Stop and think for a moment: How would you feel if you got home this evening and found three phone calls waiting for you—three calls from prospective employers eager to talk to you about putting your time and talent to work for them? Quite a different feeling from getting turned down, isn't it?

Now let's pause for a moment and analyze the Gold Form.

The Gold Form and How and Why It Works

At the back of this book you'll find two sample Gold Forms that you can adapt to your own needs. And along with Joe's Gold Form, you'll find Gold Forms used by our students Linda Turner, Donna Miller, and Linda Smith, whose experiences we'll tell you about a bit later.

Another recent student of ours called the Gold Form a "sales tool." We thought, "Hmmmm. He could be right." Thinking about it further, we said, "That's it—AICDC!"

ALL ABOUT AICDC

In every course in professional salesmanship the letters
AICDC come up. They stand for:

Attention,
Interest,
Conviction,
Desire, and
Close.

These five words represent the five steps to selling anything. And of course we're talking about selling the greatest product going—*you!*

A = Attention

The Gold Form gets the prospective employer's attention first with its color and second with the headline
"Available Immediately." As I explained to Joe, the sharp-
est contrast in colors is *not* black on white, but black on
bright yellow (or gold). Think for just a moment. What
color are all the school buses in America painted? A highly
visible bright yellow—to protect our most precious assets,
our children! What color are most fire engines painted?
Either red or, recently, a bright yellow or chartreuse!

Recently I was a guest on a talk show in southern
California. The previous guest was running over and I was
told, "Hold on, we'll be with you in five minutes."

The previous guest was talking on the subject of color.
She worked with a group called the Color Institute of

America (or some similar name). She was making the point that color sells. She told of a survey the institute had done. It had mailed out 10,000 letters on white paper and got about 100 responses. When the institute mailed out 10,000 letters on blue paper it got 112 responses; when it used pink paper it received 124 responses. But when the institute mailed out 10,000 letters on goldenrod paper it received 142 responses—a whopping 42 percent greater return than was achieved with white paper.

I = Interest

The "interest" step is accomplished by calling the employer's attention to the fact that you are qualified, experienced, dependable, and responsible. It's important to note here that you should send your "bookkeeper form" *only* to businesses that would need a bookkeeper, and a "salesperson form" *only* to businesses that would need salespersons. Makes sense, doesn't it?

C = Conviction

In selling, the "conviction" step is completed by giving the prospective customer enough facts to convince him or her that you know what you're talking about. In Joe's case, his list of presses, cameras, cutters, and so on, that he can operate is proof enough.

As you'll have noticed when you looked at Joe's Gold Form, it lists the A. B. Dick 360 press and the A. B. Dick 360CD press. We asked Joe, "What's the difference between a 360 and a 360CD?" Joe said the "CD" stands for "chain delivery," and that most people in graphics and printing would understand that a press with chain delivery would print faster, print on two sides, and offer other features. It pays to use the jargon or buzzwords of the business you want to be in.

D = Desire

The "desire" step in selling means that you're putting the prospective customer (in this case the employer) in the position of wanting to use your service or product *(you)*. On the sample Gold Form headed "Available Immediately," look again to the section titled "Your Company Will Gain." The four items mentioned are music to the ears of every employer.

Just ask yourself the question, "What employer wouldn't want an experienced _____? (Fill in the blank with your own job title.) What employer wouldn't want a dependable person who wants to work? And what would it mean to you, if you were an employer, to have a "responsible individual" who would put out valuable work? And last, the magic phrase, "A lower turnover rate," makes *you* the answer to an employer's dreams.

C = Close

No sales presentation is complete unless the salesperson *(you) asks for the order.* The Gold Form does so effortlessly by asking the employer to "help solve your problems today" by calling _____ (*your* number. Note that the Gold Form does not say: "Help solve *my unem-ployment problems*.")

And if that's not enough, the Gold Form repeats, "and I'm available immediately."

There you have the magic of the Gold Form. It works!

We use AICDC, the five great rules of selling, on a regular basis in all our work and our dealings with people. They are part of our life, and they came to the forefront naturally when Joe designed the Gold Form to help his son get a job. The tools you learn in selling yourself for the job of your dreams can be applied to any area of your life, to get what you want.

Now reread the discussion of AICDC. Get it firmly planted in your mind. You'll gain additional understanding of the way the Gold Form works as you ask yourself, "How can *I* use this in *my* situation?"

Now, for another successful example, turn to "Linda Turner's Gold Form" in the back of the book. With Linda's form you'll be able to follow the AICDC formula to the letter.

Linda believed enough in the formula to try it. She is now a successful sales representative with a large computer firm in Houston. Linda Turner is doing *exactly what she wants to do.*

She was living in Denver when she made the decision to change fields. She wanted to go into sales, and she was willing to relocate.

Linda Turner's Gold Form is an excellent model if you want to change fields completely. As you read and reread Linda's form, ask yourself, "What did Linda previously do for a living?"

The answer: We don't know. And we'll bet you too will have a hard time analyzing her past. The Gold Form stresses *not* what you have done previously, but rather, what you *want* to do *now*—and, more specifically, what's in it for the company.

Now *you* are ready to take the first big step in allowing yourself to do what *you* want to do.

Turn to the sample Gold Forms (printed on white paper) at the back of the book. The forms are headed "Available Immediately" and "Meet _____!"

With these forms in hand, start filling in the blanks with the answers that apply to *you*. This is your chance to toot your own horn. It's your opportunity to tell an employer on paper what he or she will gain by hiring you.

It's your chance to "go outside the lines."

Congratulations—you're on your way!

And now let's talk about where to send your completed Gold Forms.

THE WORLD'S LARGEST JOB-OPENING LIST

What is the largest job-opening list in the world?

It's simply a list of *every* business in your city or the city in which you want to work. As we said earlier when we talked about Lynn, who landed her Perfect Job by Interviewing for Information, the most readily available directory of all businesses is the Yellow Pages.

If you've decided you want to work in the city you now live in, a local Yellow Pages is at your fingertips. But what about other cities? Where can you find those Yellow Pages?

There are two answers to that question:

1. Your main library has a phone directory section. Call and ask whether the section has a phone directory for the city you're interested in.
2. The phone company's main office has a file of phone books from all across the United States. Call and ask where the company's library of phone books is located.

The advantage of using the public library's phone books is that the library also has photocopy machines. Since you can't check out the directories, you may want to photocopy the pages you need.

SPECIALIZED DIRECTORIES

Besides the Yellow Pages, a wealth of more specialized directories exists. Your best friend in researching these directories will be the librarian at the main library in your city. Instead of just walking into the library and spending time trying to find what you want, allow the librarian to do what he or she does best—helping you get what you need. Your librarian can help you become familiar with the tremendous resources available to you.

When you go to the library, plan to spend several hours there. Going first to the business reference section, enlist the help of the librarian to become acquainted with the various directories. Ask lots of questions. You may want to prepare a list of questions to take with you about the information you would like to find.

Pat K. was a bookkeeper/secretary in Lakewood, Colorado. When we asked what she *really* wanted to do, she replied, "I'd like to be a sales representative." We said, "Fantastic, Pat, there's a terrific demand for female sales reps." She went on, "I'm not done yet, Joe—I'd like to be a sales representative selling pharmaceuticals!"

Frowning, Joe asked her, "Pat, do you have a four-year degree? Pharmaceutical sales reps, he knew, needed that four-year degree.

She said, "As a matter of fact I don't. I only have a two-year degree." She went on to say that she wanted to sell pharmaceuticals *only to veterinarians.*

Pat knew *exactly* what she wanted.

She prepared the Gold Form. Even though we have always referred to our form as the Gold Form, Pat decided she wanted to use blue paper. At this point in our classes and seminars we did not have the benefit of research on the impact of various colors on response. Our students were using a variety of color. The important thing at this point was to use color, not white, buff, or ivory. Pat was kind enough to send us a copy—and then we lost track of her until about a month later, when we received a note saying, "Joe, thank you for helping me get the job I've *always wanted.*"

Joe had to find out what she was up to. He called her and asked if they could have lunch together.

She replied that it was kind of late for that, as she had sold her furniture and in two days was leaving Colorado for Iowa and then Illinois.

"Wait," Joe said, "tell me what's happening."

The following is Pat K.'s report of her experiences in getting the job she really wanted.

Joe, do you remember the Gold Form you told us about in your class? And the instructions that came with it? Well, I followed them to a T, except that I wanted my form on blue paper.

Next I went to the library and asked for a directory of pharmaceutical companies that deal primarily with veterinarians. The librarian was so helpful in finding one that fit my specifications perfectly.

I found a directory with sixty-two companies in it that sell pharmaceuticals to veterinarians.

I mailed out sixty-two of the blue forms. A week later I received three replies. I talked with the first company by phone and eliminated it right away.

The second company was in St. Louis, and they sent me a plane ticket to fly from Denver to St. Louis to interview with them. We were interested in one another and agreed to put each other on hold.

Company number three is in Fort Dodge, Iowa. They flew me there for an interview. I liked them. They liked me. They hired me.

I leave Lakewood day after tomorrow for Fort Dodge, Iowa. I will spend two weeks there training and going through the company plant. Afterward they will relocate me to Peoria, Illinois.

In Peoria I will be in charge of half the state of Illinois. They are giving me a company car and a company expense account. I will be on the road four days a week.

Incidentally, Pat is twenty-eight years old and single and loves it.

At this point Joe said, "Stop, Pat! How were you able to get this job with only two years of college?"

"That's the neatest thing about this, Joe," Pat said. *"The company is going to pay for me to get the rest of my education!"*

That day, our student Pat really taught Joe something.

Question: Do you need a four-year degree to get a job selling pharmaceuticals? Answer: Yes!

Next question: Do you need the degree *before* or *after* you get the job? Answer: We don't know. Why not find out?

Let's analyze the way Pat got exactly what she wanted.

1. Pat *believed* that the Gold Form worked.
2. Pat was willing to fill out the blank form ("Available Immediately . . .") and tailor it to her particular situation.
3. Pat enlisted the help of a librarian to find the exact directory to help her accomplish the next step.
4. Pat mailed sixty-two blue forms and got three replies.

Are you willing to take steps 1 through 4?
You too can have employers calling you? How?

Do it! Do it right! And do it right now!

THE ASSOCIATION FOR ASSOCIATIONS

You may be wondering why we told you Pat K.'s story in so much detail.

First we related the story of Joe's son and his request for a printer's job, which we thought was about as general a job as you can find. Then we told you about Pat K.'s request for a very specific (unusual) job.

Somewhere between the very general job goal of becoming a printer and the highly specific goal of getting a job as a pharmaceutical sales rep for a company that only deals with veterinarians, your own story should fit.

Here's where your librarian can help you again. In America we're so well organized that we have a *Directory of Directories,* published by Gale.

We even have an association for associations. It's called the American Society of Association Executives. And we have a four-volume directory called Gale's *Encyclopedia of Associations,* which lists more than 22,000 U.S. associations.

Here's how you can track down associations that can help you. Whatever city you live in, pick up your Yellow Pages. Turn to the A's and find "Associations."

In Denver we have more than 475 associations. Cities such as Los Angeles, Chicago, New York, and Washington, D.C., have even more. So you'll want to take the next step and ask your librarian (you should be getting to know him or her as a friend by now) for the *Directory of Directories* and the *Encyclopedia of Associations.*

Scan the list. Isn't it amazing how many associations there are in allied fields? Now go over the list carefully and look for the ones you're interested in.

Let's pause here and go back over the four keys that Pat K. used to become a sales representative for a pharmaceutical firm dealing with veterinarians.

Pat didn't stop at researching the field. She didn't stop at creating her blue form. She went all the way through step 4 and *mailed out* sixty-two of the blue forms.

And as important as all four steps in this process are, we're firmly convinced that the key word that helped Pat get what she wanted is the word

Believe

At every step along the way Pat *believed* that she was entitled to enjoy herself in the job that she wanted.

She *believed* that the idea of the Gold Form (or blue form) worked.

She *believed* that filling out the blank form was the next logical step in focusing her energy on what she wanted.

She also *believed* that libraries were in a position to help people. And she accepted their help.

And, finally, Pat *believed* in herself. She *believed* in herself enough to follow through with each step of the process necessary to get the job she *really* wanted, including mailing out her own blue forms.

One of our proudest possessions is a business card that Pat left with us on a recent return visit to Denver. It read:

Pat K_____
Sales Representative
Fort Dodge Laboratories
Fort Dodge, Iowa

with her home address and phone number in Peoria, Illinois.

And Then There Was Donna . . .

Here's a letter we received about two weeks after we met Donna Miller.

Joe,

Thank you for your help and the knowledge you shared on the subject of "How to Get the Job You *Really*

Want." Because of the knowledge that I gained, I can write you of my success in finding another job.

I had my doubts about how well I would do using your system of the flyers and the phone book, but I now apologize for having any doubts. I had used the want ads for several months and had little luck.

July 16th I will start my new job for Rocky Mountain Export Company as a bookkeeper/secretary. I will be working in a totally nonsmoking office. My main reason for wanting to change jobs is that I have become very sensitive to smoke in the past fourteen months, and have lost my voice a total of seven times for over four months due to the smoke in the present office.

As you can see by my flyer I stated very plainly that I wanted a nonsmoking office. I was afraid that I was going to eliminate myself from too many places by stating my need, but medically for me it was a necessity to find a nonsmoking office. To my surprise, I received two responses to the thirty flyers that I mailed out. The job that I accepted was from the first seven flyers that I mailed.

The cost of my job hunting was very inexpensive. When I compared it to what it would have cost me to go through an employment agency, well, there is no comparison.

Thank you so much, again. I totally believe in your system. If I can find a job with my special need, anyone should be able to find one. *I forgot to tell you that this company was not looking for anyone until they saw my flyer.* I will also be making $50 more a month to start. Again, thanks and bless you.

Sincerely,
Donna Miller

Look for Donna Miller's Gold Form at the back of the book.

In summary: After we've made a decision about the kind of job we want, the next step is to prepare the Gold Form. This form will be our advertising tool. It advertises the best product we have to offer: ourselves.

When we've prepared the Gold Form, it's time for us to decide *whom to send it to.*

We need to decide whether we want to continue to live in the city we live in now, or whether we're willing to relocate to do what we want to do.

Once we've made that decision, we can get the names of businesses that need our service or expertise from the Yellow Pages in our own city or another city. And we can go to the library and get lists of such companies in the area of the country we want to work in.

One secret of this method is to *send the Gold Forms out in volume.* At least 100 of the forms need to be mailed. This method is called the shotgun approach. (We will discuss the rifle approach in the next section.) The shotgun approach will get anywhere from a 5 percent to a 20 percent return.

More examples follow of the results people have gotten with the Gold Form.

People Like Linda Smith Really Use Their Creativity

Linda had been a successful schoolteacher for fifteen years. Then she worked for several years in financial planning.

In fact, things were going so well that Linda went out on her own.

One day she called and said, "Joe, help me get a job."

"What kind of job are you looking for?" Joe asked.

Linda didn't hesitate. "I want to be a wholesaler!"

She described the work of a wholesaler. She would work directly for a large syndicator, conducting seminars for large financial institutions across the country, thereby using her teaching skills as well as her knowledge of the financial industry.

Linda saw the Gold Form for Linda Turner and asked, "Could I use that idea? It's almost exactly what I'd want to write about myself." She designed her Gold Form and changed the details to suit her situation.

Next she found a directory that listed more than 600 real estate syndicators. She prepared and sent out a mailing to *all those companies.*

Joe said, "Linda, that's going to be a lot of postage!" (Like father, like son.)

About a week after she had sent out her Gold Forms, Joe called Linda and asked, "What's happening?" She said, "Nothing. I'm afraid I'm not getting any results."

A week later Linda called to report that a company in Salt Lake City had called her and had flown her to Salt Lake for an interview. But upon returning to Denver she decided to put this company on hold pending other responses.

The next week Joe got another call from Linda. "I just returned from San Jose, California, where a second company made me a good offer. But I'm still not quite sure."

Week number four: An excited Linda called Joe and said:

I've got to tell you about the exciting thing that happened to me. A man called from Milwaukee, Wisconsin, and said, "Linda, my daughter is looking for a job. Can she use the Gold Form idea also?" I assured him that it was O.K. with me.

He continued, "If everything you put on your Gold Form is true"—and I assured him that everything was true—"I'd like for you to go to work for me."

I said, "You're number three on my list. I've already got two job offers."

He countered with, "What would it take for me to be number one?"

What a nice position to be in, wouldn't you agree?
Linda went on:

I answered that first of all, I wanted to go to work for a large, stable company. He assured me that his company was one of the largest in the industry.

He had me fly out to Pasadena, California, to tour their home office and assure myself that they were large *and* stable.

Upon my return I called him and said, "Second, I want to work for someone who is willing to train me. I've never been a wholesaler before."

He then had me fly to Florida to spend a whole week with one of his top wholesalers. I followed this person around and wrote down everything he said, and even watched what he ate for breakfast.

When I returned I called my Milwaukee employer. And now it was his turn to ask questions. "Linda," he said, "you now have to choose between St. Louis, Missouri, and Kansas

City, Missouri, because Denver and Colorado are not part of my territory."

When I asked him the difference between St. Louis and Kansas City he told me that St. Louis had the better Italian restaurants. And on that basis my daughter and I are relocating to St. Louis to begin an exciting adventure with a new job in a new city.

Exciting because the first year, instead of earning twenty-eight to thirty thousand dollars as a schoolteacher or financial planner, I will be earning between seventy-five and eighty thousand dollars. Wow! What an exciting turn of events.

And to make it even more exciting, I received about ten more job offers, which I immediately gave to friends of mine who were also hunting for their Perfect Job.

You'll notice that Linda Smith's Gold Form is somewhat similar to Linda Turner's. This just shows you that you don't have to reinvent the wheel but can be creative enough to adapt what has worked for other people to your own needs.

Researching a Company That You Want to Work For

Perhaps you know exactly what you want to do and whom you want to work for. When you can be *this specific* about what you want, we call it the *rifle approach*.

When you know whom you want to work for, the

important thing is to research the company and get all the knowledge you can about it. Then go to the company and tell the bosses you want to work for them. Yes, that's right:

Ask for the job.

Researching a company is very easy. Again, you can go to the library and find annual reports on all large companies that contain a wealth of information.

Another way is to call the company and Interview for Information. Receptionists are the greatest resource— they know all about the company.

Prepare an inventory of questions. The following could serve as a guide:

How long have you been in business?
In what geographic area do you do business?
What is the most important task that you do?
Do you have any literature about your company that
   you could send me?

Questions like these can assist you in becoming as familiar as possible with the company.

Remember that receptionists like recognition too, so be friendly. Generally, people will respond to you in the same manner in which you approach them.

USING THE INFORMATION YOU GAIN FOR YOUR COMPETITIVE ADVANTAGE

The information you gain can also be used in the job interview. Include facts in the interview by making remarks such as, "I'm really excited about working for a company like yours. I noticed that last year you had a twenty-seven-percent increase in sales. Again this year you're way ahead of projections."

This type of statement is music to an employer's ears. He or she knows that you have the company's interest at heart and don't want just a paycheck.

ANSWERING A QUESTION WITH A QUESTION

In teaching a class on selling at Arapahoe Community College (near Denver), Joe tells his students, "The person who asks the questions controls the situation." This is called the Socratic method.

This concept is not only important in the interview process, but it is the most effective way to let your prospective employer know that you're participating fully in the interview.

When the interviewer asks, "Do you have a résumé?" your response could be, "Is a résumé necessary?" Should the interviewer reply, "Yes, we need a résumé from each applicant," it would be appropriate to continue by asking, "What type of résumé would you like? Chronological or functional?" By using these questions in this sequence, you may find that the employer only wants you to fill out the company's employment application.

If you're already in the employer's office, he or she may interview you based on your Gold Form.

Carol, a recent graduate of our jobs seminar, told us that she had stopped by the placement office of Denver University. She had received her M.B.A. from DU.

The placement officer said, "Carol, we don't have your résumé in our M.B.A. grad file!"

Carol said she hadn't known that the office maintained an M.B.A. grad file. She went home and spent several weeks preparing the "perfect résumé." She used an IBM Selectric typewriter and took the finished product to the print shop to be printed rather than photocopied. Then she proudly returned to the placement office with her new résumé.

The placement officer shook his head, saying, "Oh, no, Carol! We need your résumé *typeset,* not typewritten!"

Another $60 plus down the drain for Carol. And she lost another three weeks.

Our advice is: Find out what is *actually required* before investing your time and money in résumés.

In Summary

Do you remember seeing the movie or the play *Auntie Mame?* We sit through the performance each time to hear the closing remarks: *"Life is a banquet. But most SOB's are starving to death!"*

Life *is* a series of choices, isn't it?

We heard a friend say, "We are where we are because we chose to be there!"

Think about the smallest decisions first. You may want to answer these questions:

Who chose the outfit you're wearing today?
Who chose the last meal you ate?
Who chose the house or apartment you live in?

Granted, some of these may have been joint decisions, but don't you agree that *you are in charge of your life?*

Now, may we ask, who chose the job or career you're in today? Who chose the company you work for today? And who chose the city in which you work?

ARE YOU WHERE YOU WANT TO BE?

Richard Bolles asks three vital questions in *What Color Is Your Parachute?* (Ten Speed Press, 1972):

1. What do you want to do (occupationally)?
2. Where do you want to do it (geographically)?
3. Who do you want to do it for (individually within the company)?

We believe that if you can answer these three questions *in detail* you're well on the road to getting what you want out of life.

Picture this: You go to the airport in your hometown. You walk up to the ticket counter. The airline clerk asks,

"Where would you like to go?" Just imagine the expression on the clerk's face if you say, "Anywhere, it doesn't matter." Where do you think the clerk will give you a ticket to?

Have you ever tried to mail a letter without a complete address? It will land right back in your mailbox for more complete instructions.

Now try this for fun. Go into a restaurant. When the waitperson asks for your order, just tell him or her you want something "good," something "nourishing," and watch his or her expression. What will probably happen is that the waitperson will smile and give you a second chance before throwing you out.

On the other hand, when you confidently walk up to the airline counter and tell the clerk you want to go to Washington, D.C., the only other question that will be asked is, "Which airport would you like to fly into?"

When the waitperson asks for your order and you ask for a sirloin steak, medium rare, you will get a sirloin steak, medium rare. And so it is with the question "Which job do you really want?" You will get exactly what you ask for.

And you will get the job you really want *faster* not only when you ask for it, but when you *believe* that it is yours and *act* upon the ideas in this book.

WHAT WE THINK ABOUT, WE BRING ABOUT

We are constantly talking to ourselves. As you've been reading this book, you've been talking to yourself at the same time. As new ideas have passed before your eyes, you've made judgments about them. You may have said, "Great!" or, "Oh, no, that will never work."

Whatever we say to ourselves becomes our reality.

Here are several affirmations—positive things to say to yourself—which will help you get positive results. Copy them onto three-by-five cards. Carry one in your wallet or purse and read it daily. Put one over the sun visor of your car and read it daily. Put one on the bathroom mirror and read it daily.

**IF YOU THINK YOU CAN OR YOU THINK YOU CAN'T,
YOU ARE RIGHT . . .**

**WORDS RUN THROUGH THE MIND
REPETITIOUSLY
INEVITABLY
BECOME REALITY!**

**THE THINGS I SEEK
ARE SEEKING ME
AND WE SHALL
COME TOGETHER!**

As we said, we human beings have been talking to ourselves all our lives. But most of what we've been feeding into the computers in our heads has been garbage. We've been telling ourselves that we're not good enough to have that raise in pay, or that job we've always wanted. Or that we're not self-confident enough, or pretty enough, or young enough, or old enough.

What have you been telling yourself?

You see, your subconscious mind doesn't know the

difference between something real and something imagined. It will bring you anything you tell it to.

The conscious mind is the thinker, and the subconscious mind is the prover. It will prove that anything we say to ourselves is right.

For example, if we believe that people around us are always mean to us, that's what our experience will be. If our subconscious did not prove to us that we're right, we would go crazy. Imagine believing that people are mean and then experiencing people being nice to you.

The real key is to feed into our minds *what it is that we want.*

What we're talking about is using positive affirmations—repeating to ourselves positive phrases in the present tense about the things we want to have happen in our lives. Here are some examples:

I am self-confident.

I am worthy of the job I want.

I am creative.

My perfect job is waiting for me.

I use my time wisely.

I have a multitude of friends.

I am accepted and acknowledged by others.

I am in my perfect relationship.

What are some of *your* desires? Write them down. Make sure they follow the format—positive and present tense. Repeat them daily. The more times you repeat them, the better. What you're doing is reprogramming your mind. Whatever it was you were thinking must be removed and replaced with the new affirmations.

Remember, this is not something new. We all have been affirming for our entire lives. The only thing different now is that *we are paying attention to what we are saying,* inputting positive, true information about ourselves.

PART THREE

How to Turn Every Job Interview into a Job Offer

Interviewing

The time has come.

The interview has been confirmed.

This is the big day.

Either you can be scared and fill your mind with "What if" and "If only," or you can choose to be confident, poised, and prepared.

Here are some rules to help you make this interview a successful one:

1. Be sure you know where you're going and how to get there. Be early for the appointment. You want to be able to walk into the office at precisely the correct time, or better yet, ten to fifteen minutes ahead of time.
2. Be sure to dress properly for the interview. Many dress-for-success books tell you to dress for the interview as though you were applying for a job one notch higher than the one you are actually going for. The way you dress for the interview has nothing to

do with how you dress for the job. At the interview you're selling yourself. You need to be packaged as well as possible.

There are three other elements critical to this interview, three elements which we all need if we're to be successful:

1. a good, firm handshake,
2. good eye contact, and
3. a prepared list of questions.

Women sometimes wonder what to do about the handshake: Always be the first to put out your hand. Men are sometimes confused about what to do when meeting a woman: Always put out your hand. This is the rule in business situations.

A good, firm handshake and eye contact tell a person a lot about your confidence level. This is how people read us. If you feel a little weak in these areas, practice shaking hands and maintaining good eye contact until you feel comfortable.

Be sure to prepare a list of questions on a pad or in a notebook before going to the interview. List everything you want to know about the job. These questions should not be limited to those like "When would my vacation be?" They could include:

"Who will be my immediate supervisor?"
"What specific training will I get?"
"What training opportunities does the company provide for possible advancement to other positions?"
"What happened to the person who previously had this position?"

"How frequently will my work performance be reviewed?"

Most people believe that an interview is over when either the applicant or the employer has run out of questions. After you're satisfied that you and your prospective employer have answered all the questions that you've posed to each other, take the following steps:

1. Stop.
2. Summarize.
3. Close.

Simply *stop* the Ping-Pong game by asking the employer, "Is there anything else that you want to know about me and my qualifications at our first interview?"

If the employer answers no, *summarize* by reviewing your background, experience, and qualifications. For example: "Mr./Ms. Employer, I feel that with my background, education, and experience, I would do a good job for your organization. This could help us both reach our goals."

Finally, *close* with the following statement and question: "I'm available immediately. How soon would you want me to start?" Then be quiet and listen for the answer.

As you might suspect, very few people ask for what they want. By using the stop-summarize-close technique, you'll put yourself in the top 1 percent because you've *asked for the order.*

If selling yourself feels awkward or foreign, practice in front of a mirror or with a friend playing the part of the employer. Keep doing this until you're comfortable with yourself and the results.

We've interviewed hundreds of employers, always asking them the same questions: "What are you really looking for? What would make you hire one applicant over all the rest?"

These employers have almost always answered with the same words: "I'm looking for someone who is willing to *ask for the job!*"

Is it that simple? Just about!

Thirty Ways to Ask for the Job

Joe was invited to speak to fifty seniors at Cherry Creek High School near Denver early one morning. After giving them a forty-five-minute overview of the materials in our seminars, he concluded by telling them about the stop-summarize-close technique we've just introduced.

Joe said the kids wanted to crawl under their desks. The teacher saved the day by putting her hand on Joe's shoulder and saying, "Mr. Sabah, I believe that your technique would be a bit too heavy for our students to use. I'll tell you what: Our class will come up with ways they could 'ask for the job' and we'll send you a list of our ideas."

Here they are, all Thirty Ways to Ask for the Job:

1. When would you like me to start?
2. Where will I work?

3. Who will be my boss?
4. When would you like me to meet some of my coworkers?
5. Thank you for the interview; I would really like to have this job.
6. It would really be nice to have this job.
7. Do you think I have a chance for the job?
8. The office, benefits, etc., are super; I think I would like to make my career here.
9. Do I have the job?
10. I can start as soon as possible.
11. I can start today if you want.
12. I will do my very best for your company.
13. I would be very happy working here.
14. The office seems like a pleasant place to work.
15. Both you and I can gain.
16. What time should I be here?
17. Thank you; I hope I will be working with you and others.
18. What time tomorrow would you like me to come in?
19. Will I be working Monday through Friday?
20. How many employees do you have now?
21. Will I be typing and answering the phone?
22. I think I would be a good asset to your company.
23. I can't wait to start working here.
24. I hope I'll get along with all your other employees.
25. When can I call back to find out when I can start?
26. If possible, could I help make coffee in the morning as a contribution to the office?
27. During the first week, can I look around and familiarize myself with the office and how it runs?

28. Will I be in charge of locking up?
29. Do you feel I am qualified for this job?
30. Will I be working full-time or part-time?

And Joe thought he was being assertive!

Here's how you can use this information. We believe that out of these Thirty Ways to Ask for the Job, you'll be able to find one or two good closing questions. Pick out the best one or two and practice, practice, practice. First practice with friends or family. Next, use your closing question in *every* interview you have. Asking for the job works!

How to Get Your Name to the Top of the List

Here is a technique that will either get you the job after the first interview or put your name at the top of the list.

After the interview is over, regardless of the outcome, do not go home. Instead, go directly to the nearest post office (not a mailbox) and write out a thank-you note. You're going right to the post office so that the note will be delivered the next day, or as soon as possible after your interview.

You can write your note on a card without any printed words, except for "Thank You," or on regular writing paper. A store-bought thank-you card is not as effective. Here are three rules to guide your thank-you note writing:

1. All thank-you notes should be handwritten.
2. Your thank-you note should be mailed before 5 P.M. so that your future employer will receive it first thing the next morning.
3. Your note should state your thanks, restate your qualifications, and finally *ask for the job* again.

Here's a sample letter:

Thank you very much, Ms. Jones, for the time you shared with me today discussing my career possibilities with XYZ Company. I feel that with my experience, education, and background, I would be able to help you to accomplish your department goals for this year. I'm enthusiastically looking forward to being part of your team.

> Sincerely,
> Fred Jobhunter

Do this and we promise that, regardless of how many applicants there are for the position, your name will move to the top of the list. Why? Because you're unique. You took the time to write a thank-you note! A small item, maybe—but oh so powerful.

Congratulations again! *You are a winner!*

On the following pages are some of the many reports we've received from individuals who have used the ideas and methods we have described in this book—*success stories*. Read on! We're positive that one or more of these stories will spark the creativity in your mind and help *you* put these ideas into practice *now!*

PART FOUR

Success Stories

Andy Negotiated a Raise Before He Started Work

A former student named Andy wrote to Joe:

> Here's how I improved myself from being unemployed to a good job with decent salary and good opportunity for self-development. I answered an ad for the March of Dimes to help with their Mothers' March. I talked with the Exec (not the person who normally would have interviewed for the position). I was told that I more or less appeared to lack confidence in myself and that I was either overqualified or differently qualified for the job.
>
> The next day I got a call from the Exec telling me that they were going to create a position for Education Program Coordinator. Not being overly impressed with the organization so far, I went and talked to him about the job. He was interested in the fact that I had mentioned the possibility of Voc-Rehab picking up the tab for my salary due to my hearing loss. The original salary was rather low I thought.
>
> During the next few weeks, I began more active job

searching techniques and kept his offer on hold. When I learned he was willing to negotiate the salary I went back and he upped it, and I negotiated for somewhat more a month. After two weeks Voc-Rehab approved the contract. I started to work. I was pretty pleased with the salary negotiated on my part. . . . I was straight with him. . . . I didn't demand [a certain salary], but simply stated what I needed and what I was worth.

So thanks to the information I received from you, I got the job I wanted. I also see unlimited potential in the future to create my own job.

Affirmation: I Ask for What I Want and Get What I Deserve.

Doug Got His Dream Job with Disney World

A young man named Doug reported on his success with the Gold Form:

I am a junior at a small midwestern college in Iowa who, thanks to you and the "Gold Form," will be going through Walt Disney's college program this summer.

Four weeks ago I received a flyer in my school mailbox telling me about "The Disney College Program." It said that two reps from Disney would be out to the state of Iowa and would be looking for juniors in college majoring in the field of business; if interested talk to Sue Jones in the career development office on campus. I was interested so I went to speak with her. She gave me an application to fill out and told me the time and place of the interview. She said that a lot of students would probably be applying and that the Disney reps would be looking for only a few people.

So then I knew I had to come up with something really unique so that the two reps would remember me. I then remembered reading about the Gold Form in your book. I thought that was a great idea, especially after reading success stories of the Gold Form. My friends (some of them anyway) thought I was a little crazy, not only for using the Gold Form, but also for trying for a position with Disney. I believed I could do it.

The Gold Form worked like a charm during the interview (no one else had one). Two weeks later I received a letter from Disney saying that they would like to have me join them as a Fast Food Host with the Walt Disney College Program.

The Gold Form gave me the unique edge that put me a cut above the rest in order to receive the position.

DOUG'S GOLD FORM

AVAILABLE FOR SUMMER/FALL PROGRAM

Doug Rand is a creative, honest, positive, quick to learn, and hard-working young man.

I have been very active during my past three years in college.

- Elected Fraternity President for the 87–88 school year.
- Elected Psychology Vice President for 86–88 school years.
- A Resident Advisor for 86–88 school years.
- Two-year letter winner in cross country and also in track.
- Member of my dorm's governing body.
- I am also maintaining a 3.1 overall G.P.A.; my studies are very important to me.

Qualified. . . . Strong People Background and People Skills in
Knowing When and How to Listen
Motivating Others
Keeping a Positive Attitude, Even When the Chips Seem to Be Down
Following Through on My Commitments to Others
Knowing When to Be a Leader and When to Be a Follower

I will graduate from Cornell College in 1988 with a Bachelor of Arts. My Major is Economics, and my Minor is Psychology.

YOUR COMPANY WILL GAIN:
- A dependable person
- A person who has had a multitude of business courses
- A person who <u>REALLY</u> wants to work and learn through your college business management program
- An outstanding future employee
- A very flexible person who can easily adjust to any situation

It would be an honor and a privilege to be accepted into the WALT DISNEY COLLEGE PROGRAM. Thank you for considering me as a candidate. If I am accepted into your program (either summer or fall), I promise you that I won't let you down.
Please Send the Letter of Acceptance to:
  Doug Rand
  1234 Gold Road
  Montrose, IL 12345

My Motto Is—"Man Who Says 'It Can't Be Done' Should Not Interrupt Man Doing It."

Bob Generated Temporary Income While He Searched for His Ideal Job

Our student Bob wrote:

I used the "Dear Belcaro Residents," to generate temporary self-employment in my neighborhood. So far, good results, distributing 300 copies in doors. I included some of your ideas. Still looking at other permanent career choices in financial non-accounting areas.

Bob's Gold Form is on the following page.

BOB'S GOLD FLYER

DEAR BELCARO RESIDENTS

Do you need personal services performed by someone who is organized, dependable, honest, hard-working, competent, friendly, and flexible on working hours?

A. Home

   1. Leaves raked
   2. Windows washed
   3. Maintenance and repairs
   4. Trees and shrubs trimmed
   5. Snow shoveled
   6. Errands or shopping (Christmas) done
   7. Home- or pet-sitting services
   8. Car waxed

B. Business

   1. Income tax prep. or assistance
   2. Accounting system for small business
   3. Financial planning or consulting
   4. Consumer advice—comparisons

C. Photography

   1. Portraits—family, individuals, pets
   2. Home and personal property
   3. Commercial
   4. Christmas cards

Affirmation: I Use My Creative Mind in Many Ways.

Bill Didn't Need an Appointment (A Flower Helped, Though)

Bill wanted to work for a particular airline because they fly to Hawaii. He researched the company and found out the name of the personnel manager (Mr. F. Gay).

Putting on his best suit, Bill visited the personnel office and said, "May I speak with Mr. Gay, please?"

The secretary said, "Just a moment, I'll see if he's in."

In a few moments she came back and said, "Bill, Mr. Gay is in and available to see you now."

Bill had a delightful visit with Mr. Gay and told him he had always wanted to work for an airline, especially this one. Mr. Gay said that of course Bill would have to fill out an application.

Mr. Gay took Bill back to the front desk and asked the secretary to give Bill an application. Thanking Mr. Gay, Bill then asked the secretary her name, accepted the application, and said good-bye.

Bill returned in two days with the filled-out application and a single red rose for the secretary. He handed her the application; she said, "Just a moment, I think Mr. Gay would like to see you."

Bill got a second interview with Mr. Gay. In two weeks he was on his way to Los Angeles for an employment physical, and he started work in the next ten days.

What's your response to this story? Is it, "You must have an appointment for an interview." Is that true? Not necessarily.

Or is your response, "Bringing the secretary a flower, isn't that corny?" Most of us human beings are looking for recognition, and Bill provided the recognition the secretary wanted and needed. Such recognition certainly helps pave the way to better relationships in both our personal and professional lives.

We can learn two things from Bill's experience. First, *never* listen to people who say you must have an appointment. What if the secretary had said Mr. Gay wasn't in? The next step would have been either to make an appointment or to come back. What about the flower? Just good public relations!

> **Affirmation: I Give Others the Same Kind of Recognition I Like to Receive.**

Carol Learned How to Become Successfully Self-Employed

On her own business letterhead, Carol wrote to Joe:

> For years I tried working to satisfy others' goals. Hey, let me assure you it does not work.
>
> As you recall, during our counseling session, I asked you three questions concerning my entry into the field as an association director.
>
> 1. Is there a need in the marketplace?
> 2. Can I make a living doing it?

3. Knowing me, do you feel I have the qualifications to
   make a go of it?

When you showed me that the answer to all three question was *"Yes,"* and then gave me a specific plan of action to
follow to achieve my goal, I was just thrilled.

You gave me direction and the courage necessary to per-
severe, and almost before I knew it, I was achieving goals
which, previous to talking to you, I would have considered
impossible.

However, more than the career achievement is my personal happiness. I've always enjoyed working with volunteer organizations, and to think that I could turn an
avocation into a lucrative vocation is almost too good to be
true.

I have had a lot of disappointment, have learned a lot
making mistakes, am still not where I want to be, but at least
I wake up each morning knowing that the potential for joy
is there because I am pursuing a line of work which brings
me a great deal of satisfaction.

**Affirmation: I Make Money Doing the
Activities I Enjoy.**

Kathy Said, "I Was the Only Person the Company Called, and That Company Was the Only One I Wanted to Work For."

We heard from a former student named Kathy:

> I decided to heed your suggestion and prepare a flyer/résumé (Gold Form) unique to me. I mass mailed about sixty copies, then called all recipients.
>
> Unfortunately, my target population did not have funds to employ me at the time.
>
> But without exception each company made positive mention of my flyer. Everyone remembered my flyer, and many stated they put it in their "worth keeping" file, in case their company's financial status changed.
>
> Well, one company's did. (The one I wanted to work for the most!)
>
> They called me last week (the only person they called), and I start working for them next week! I can hardly wait.
>
> Thanks for your creative approaches to job hunting! They really work! Also, I learned the art of patience.

Affirmation: I Am a Unique Individual, with Persistence and Patience.

Lee Found Out It Pays to Be Persistent

Lee wrote:

Several months ago I took your class "How to Get the Job You *Really* Want." At that time I had identified what things I wanted in a job, and I knew that I wanted to work in my company's home office in Columbus, Ohio. I wanted to travel, to write, and to solve problems.

Something happened at work today that reminded me of you and the wonderfully positive feeling that I had when I left your class that day. I wanted to let you know what has happened to me since then. One thing that I remember you emphasized was to keep trying, and to not let a rejection or two stop you from pursuing your goal.

It has been four months since I took your class. I applied for the job I wanted *five times* before I was granted an interview in Ohio. When I walked into that interview, I knew I would get the job. It took months of waiting, and four rejections, but I'm moving to Columbus in ten days. My job there will consist of a great deal of writing, solving production and paper overload problems, and 50 percent travel!

Thank you for the positive feeling and reinforcement I got in your class. It was just the push I needed to get started on my way.

Affirmation: I Decide What I Want— and Then I Go After It.

Paul Made a Prime-Time TV Appearance

Several months after participating in our jobs seminar, Paul called to share the following story with us.

He said our ideas about the Gold Form had seemed too far out. But after several months of *no* work, he'd decided to give the Gold Form a try.

He had 150 copies printed up and instead of mailing them out, he decided to hand them out at the corner of 17th and California streets in downtown Denver, a very busy business intersection. In addition, he put on his best three-piece suit and had his roommate make up an A-frame sign reading: FUTURE JUNIOR EXECUTIVE FOR HIRE.

As he was telling us about handing out the 150 Gold Forms he asked, "Guess what happened? . . . Nothing!"

Depressed, Paul went home and let another month go by before deciding to try the Gold Form again. This time he had 100 copies printed, took his A-frame sign, dressed in his best suit, and went to 17th and California. But this time he remembered something that Judy had said in the seminar: "If you do what you've always done, you'll get what you've always gotten!"

So, deciding to try something different, Paul spotted a pay phone across the street. He left his sign and went to the pay phone. He dialed a number and said: "Is this the Channel Four Hotline? There seems to be a young fellow doing something unusual across the street from the Petro Lewis Building and I thought it might make a good news story."

After hanging up, he returned to his post and started

handing out the Gold Form again. Within thirty minutes a Channel 4 TV reporter was there interviewing him, asking, "What are you doing here, young fellow?"

As a result of this interview Paul appeared on the news at five, six, and ten o'clock.

What would you give to appear on TV three times in one day?

The next day Paul received one phone call—from the district manager of the Sperry Univac Company in Fort Collins, Colorado. The manager asked, "Are you the fellow who was on TV last night?"

Paul said, "Yes!"

He was invited to Fort Collins for an interview, was offered a job and then was sent to New Jersey for two months' training at company expense. Paul was excited when he called us to tell us that he was moving from Denver to Fort Collins to accept this position.

He took the idea of the Gold Form and carried it a step further. What could you do with this idea? How about adding your own creativity to the Gold Form?

Look out, world!

EPILOGUE

Yesterday is a canceled check . . . tomorrow is a promissory note . . . only today is _cash_, legal tender and spendable!

Thanks to our friend and mentor Cavett Robert for the above quote. It's a constant reminder that _today_ is the _only_ day we have.

We all know how much sand is in the bottom of the hourglass (years gone by), but not one of us knows for sure just how much sand is still left in the top. So why not take advantage of the time you have today?

1. Start searching for the "song you came to sing." You can get started by going back over this book and putting your pencil or pen to the exercises and projects you might have skimmed over. (Please "go outside the lines" and give yourself permission to write in this book. It's yours and it's paid for. So get started. Make it pay off.)
2. Next, review the IFI (Interviewing for Information) technique described on page 38.

3. Start practicing interviewing by taking a friend out to lunch. Don't forget to take your pad with questions on it. You'll love the experience.

4. Next, move on from interviewing a friend to finding another person to practice on, and then finally interview someone you don't know, but who is doing what you want to be doing.

5. Finally, review the Gold Forms in the back of the book.

> Pick out the one that best fits you.
>
> Use the sample Gold Forms on pages 106–107, or make up your own rough draft.
>
> Type up your own Gold Form.
>
> Take it to the nearest print shop and have it printed on *goldenrod paper*.
>
> Gather a list of at least 100 businesses that could use the type of person you describe on your form.
>
> Address the envelopes, fold the Gold Forms, insert, seal, and stamp the envelopes, then mail them *today!*
>
> Make sure you're home to answer the phone, or have a message number where someone else can take your calls.

You are now on your way to *getting the job you **really** want.*

OUR SUCCESS STORIES

Many of our students ask, "Where do you find the stories you tell us in your seminars?"

The answer: from people like you—people who took the time to listen to our ideas, believed in our system, and put the ideas into practice. These people have called and written to us with their success stories.

We'd like to hear from you!

As your success story unfolds, please keep track of the details in a notebook. Then type or write us a note, telling us in your own words *exactly what happened!* Please include copies of *your* Gold Form.

Write to:

Joe and Judy Sabah
P.O. Box 101330
Denver, CO 80250

Note: If your organization would like to schedule a seminar, please write to us at the address above or phone 303/722-7200.

SAMPLE GOLD FORMS

AVAILABLE IMMEDIATELY

One (1) Qualified, Experienced, Dependable, Responsible,_____.

I have done the following:

_____

_____

_____

_____

_____

Besides graduating from_____,

I have worked at_____.

My reason for making a change is_____

_____

I am_____years old,_____tall, weigh_____lbs., and am in excellent health.

YOUR COMPANY WILL GAIN

1. An experienced _____.
2. A dependable person who wants to work.
3. A responsible individual who will put out work that will_____

_____

4. A lower turnover rate, as I'm looking for a permanent position.

HELP SOLVE YOUR_____PROBLEMS TODAY

Call_____and ask for_____.

I live at_____.

AND I'M AVAILABLE IMMEDIATELY. . . . .

MEET_____ **!!!**

"**A**_____**IF I EVER MET ONE**"

(said by her former employer with over 25 years in_____)

_____ is: DYNAMIC   A RISK TAKER

                RESOURCEFUL   PERSISTENT

                HONEST   POSITIVE

                DIRECT   QUICK TO LEARN

QUALIFIED . . . STRONG PEOPLE BACKGROUND AND PEOPLE SKILLS IN

   HANDLING COMPLAINTS

   PROBLEM SOLVING

   MOTIVATING OTHERS

   KNOWING WHEN TO LISTEN

   KNOWING WHEN AND HOW TO ASK QUESTIONS

A graduate of _____ with a _____

_____ and a Minor in _____

WHY _____ ?

   $—An opportunity at an open-ended income

   Freedom—To work more than 40 hours a week

   Challenge—To take open-ended situations and make things happen

   Adventure—Taming the unknown

YOUR COMPANY WILL GAIN

   A person with a high _____ drive.

   An enhanced reputation in the business world.

   A lower turnover rate—I'm career oriented.

_____ ' _ ", attractive, _____ years old, _____, able to travel, excellent health

The potential is there waiting to be unleashed and molded into one of your company's _____! Whatever it takes I can and will do—truly a diamond in the rough!

INVEST IN YOUR COMPANY'S FUTURE TODAY!

   Call _____-_____ and ask for _____

                             _____

                             _____

107

JOE'S GOLD FORM

AVAILABLE IMMEDIATELY

One (1) Qualified, Experienced, Dependable, Responsible Printer

I have run the following equipment:

    A. B. Dick 360
    A. B. Dick 360CD
    A. B. Dick 385

    A/M Multi 1250

    Folders, several makes and models

    Agfa-Gevaert Repromaster Camera
    Cutters, both electric and hand

    A. B. Dick 133 Platemaker
    A. B. Dick 675 Platemaker

Besides graduating from the graphic classes in high school, I am working 2½ days per week in an in-house print shop.

My reason for leaving is to secure FULL-TIME employment. (My present employer knows of my desires, and has need for only part-time employment.)

I am 6'0", 165 lbs., and in excellent health.
I will be 18 in January and have graduated from high school.

YOUR COMPANY WILL GAIN
1. An experienced printer.
2. A dependable person who wants to work.
3. A responsible individual who will put out work that will bring in repeat orders.
4. A lower turnover rate, as I'm looking for a permanent position.

HELP SOLVE YOUR PRINTER PROBLEMS TODAY
Call 234-5678 and ask for Joe Sabah
I live at 1234 Willow Lane, Concord, CA 94520

AND I'M AVAILABLE IMMEDIATELY. . . . .

MEET LINDA ! ! !
"A SALESWOMAN IF I EVER MET ONE"

(said by her former employer with over 25 years in sales, who now manages a large insurance company)

Linda is: DYNAMIC   CREATIVE
           RESOURCEFUL   PERSISTENT
           HONEST   POSITIVE
           DIRECT   QUICK TO LEARN
           A RISK TAKER

QUALIFIED . . . STRONG PEOPLE BACKGROUND AND PEOPLE SKILLS IN
   HANDLING COMPLAINTS
   PROBLEM SOLVING
   MOTIVATING OTHERS
   KNOWING WHEN TO LISTEN
   KNOWING WHEN AND HOW TO ASK QUESTIONS

A graduate of the University of Illinois in 1971 with a Bachelor's in Psychology and a Minor in Math and Social Work.

WHY DIRECT SALES?
   $—An opportunity at an open-ended income
   Freedom—To work more than 40 hours a week
   Challenge—To take open-ended situations and make things
      happen
   Adventure—Taming the unknown

YOUR COMPANY WILL GAIN
   A person with a high money drive.
   An enhanced reputation in the business world.
   A lower turnover rate—I'm career oriented.

5'7", attractive, 31 years old, single, able to travel, excellent health

The potential is there waiting to be unleashed and molded into one of your company's top producers! Whatever it takes I can and will do—truly a diamond in the rough!

INVEST IN YOUR COMPANY'S FUTURE TODAY!
   Call 838-3232 and ask for Linda Turner
   2345 Skyline Drive
   Denver, CO 80200

DONNA MILLER'S GOLD FORM

WANTED NONSMOKING OFFICE

One (1) Qualified, Experienced, Responsible, Dependable, Secretary/Bookkeeper looking for a nonsmoking office.

I have the following qualifications:

    14 years general office experience
    Type 55 words per minute
    Ten key by touch
    CRT experience
    Accounts payable experience
    Accounts receivable experience
    Payroll experience
    International freight experience
    Bookkeeping through trial balance
    Willing to learn new skills

Besides attending business college, I have taken seminars and correspondence courses.

My reason for leaving my present job is to secure a job in a nonsmoking office.

YOUR COMPANY WILL GAIN

1. An experienced secretary/bookkeeper.
2. A dependable person who wants to work.
3. A responsible person whom you can trust.
4. A lower turnover rate, as I am looking for a permanent position. I have been at my present job for over five years.

Help Solve *Your* Secretary/Bookkeeping Problems Today!
Call 366-4000 or 366-0600 (Message Number)
and ask for Donna Miller
I live at 1234 Miami Way, Aurora, CO 80000

I AM AVAILABLE AND I AM WILLING TO WORK.

LINDA SMITH'S GOLD FORM

AVAILABLE . . . . IMMEDIATELY

LINDA SMITH "A saleswoman if I ever met one,"
(said by her former employer, who managed
one of Wall Street's brokerage firms)

LINDA IS:

DYNAMIC	HONEST
CREATIVE	DIRECT
INTELLIGENT	POSITIVE
RESOURCEFUL	QUICK TO LEARN
PERSISTENT	A RISK TAKER

QUALIFIED . . . SECURITIES BROKER WITH STRONG PRODUCT
  KNOWLEDGE
  . . . SPEAKING AND SEMINAR PRESENTATION SKILLS
  . . . MOTIVATING OTHERS
  . . . EFFECTIVE IN SALES AND CLOSING TECHNIQUES
** A Certified Financial Planner with a Master's in Mathematics
and extensive teaching experience **

WHY WHOLESALING?
$—AN OPPORTUNITY AT AN OPEN-ENDED INCOME
FREEDOM—TO WORK MORE THAN 40 HOURS A WEEK
CHALLENGE—TO TAKE OPEN-ENDED SITUATIONS AND
  MAKE THINGS HAPPEN.
ADVENTURE—TAMING THE UNKNOWN

YOUR COMPANY WILL GAIN
A person with a high money drive.
An enhanced reputation in the business world.
A lower turnover rate—I'm career oriented.

5'8", attractive, free to travel, willing to relocate. The potential is
there waiting to be utilized and developed into one of your company's top producers! Whatever it takes I can and will do.

INVEST IN YOUR COMPANY'S FUTURE TODAY!
CALL 303/750-0000 OR
  303/770-0000 AND ASK FOR
  LINDA SMITH
  7890 E. JACKSON PLACE
  DENVER, CO 80200

PLUME

WORKING WISDOM